WOODHEAD

COUNTDOWN
TO
CLOSURE

An illustrated survey of the final four years of operations on the Manchester-Sheffield-Wath route - the Woodhead line.

By Graham R.Jelly

BOOK LAW PUBLICATIONS

Monday 16ᵗʰ March 1981, Woodhead: Most railway photographers will be able to recall many instances when the sun disappeared at the vital moment. Much less common is the reverse. EM1s 76010 and 76016 emerge from the tunnel in a very brief flash of sunlight with a westbound train of, also less common, empties which mainly consists 24-ton hoppers.

(*Cover*) **Tuesday 10ᵗʰ February 1981, Bullhouse:** 76031 and 76033 return merry-go-round (MGR) empties to the east.

First published in the United Kingdom by
BOOK LAW PUBLICATIONS 2013
382 Carlton Hill, Nottingham, NG4 1JA
Printed and bound by The Amadeus Press, Cleckheaton, West Yorkshire.

Woodhead - Countdown to Closure

CONTENTS

Friday 17th July 1981, Elsecar Junction: 76016 and 76010 enter the yard at Wath in order to work the penultimate electrically hauled train from there.

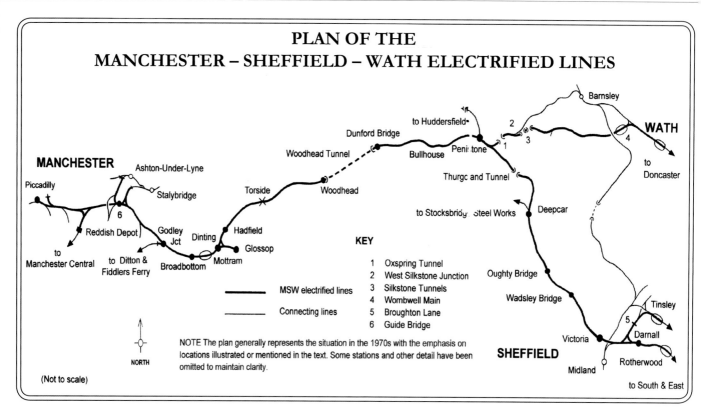

PLAN OF THE
MANCHESTER – SHEFFIELD – WATH ELECTRIFIED LINES

KEY

1 Oxspring Tunnel
2 West Silkstone Junction
3 Silkstone Tunnels
4 Wombwell Main
5 Broughton Lane
6 Guide Bridge

——— MSW electrified lines

------- Connecting lines

NORTH

NOTE The plan generally represents the situation in the 1970s with the emphasis on locations illustrated or mentioned in the text. Some stations and other detail have been omitted to maintain clarity.

(Not to scale)

Wednesday 29th October 1980, Dinting: The situation indicated with the illustration on page 2 had also occurred here when the sun came out just in time to illuminate 76051 heading east with a train of scrap metal. The former Great Central Type 5b signal box still survives.

INTRODUCTION

The first railway between Manchester and Sheffield was built by the Sheffield, Ashton-under-Lyne & Manchester Railway and opened in 1845. The route was skilfully chosen to provide a steady but relentless climb from both ends gaining approximately 750 feet to a summit at Dunford Bridge, just over midway along the 41 mile line, and 943 feet above sea level. The summit was located immediately east of the 3 mile 22 yard long, single line Woodhead tunnel, which was the most significant engineering feat on the line. The gradient profile of the line was almost perfect symmetry in the form of an inverted V with long stretches of gradients in the region of 1 in 120. Such gradients were manageable for steam locomotives but meant very hard work for both the locomotives and their crews.

After amalgamation with two railway companies having lines to the east of Sheffield, the Company became the Manchester Sheffield & Lincolnshire Railway with effect from 1st January 1847. Meanwhile, the single line tunnel on an otherwise double track line had proved to be an immediate operating inconvenience and so a second single line tunnel was constructed, opening in 1852.

One of the prime sources of traffic was coal from the South Yorkshire coalfield. A line from Barnsley to Penistone was opened in 1857. However due to the volume of traffic there was a need to by-pass Barnsley and so advantage was taken of an existing colliery branch and this, at its western extremity, was connected to the Barnsley – Penistone branch by means of a line of just over two miles, joining it at West Silkstone Junction. The convenience of this more direct route came at the considerable expense of a severe 1 in 40 gradient which became known as the Worsborough (or Wentworth) bank. Another four miles of the ten mile branch were also quite steeply graded at around 1 in 100, whilst the remainder offered no respite for westbound loaded trains. This line never carried a regular passenger service.

Due largely to the aspirations of its Chairman Sir Edward Watkin, the MS&LR looked to expand its system to London in the 1890s. In preparation for this, it built a line from east of Sheffield southwards to Annesley in Nottinghamshire. To reflect its metamorphosis from a provincial east–west railway the Company's name was changed to Great Central Railway in 1897. The so-called London Extension commenced here and reached its terminus at Marylebone via Nottingham, Leicester and Rugby. From Buckinghamshire the route was shared to within a couple of miles of Marylebone, the terminus, with the Metropolitan Railway (another company which had Watkin as Chairman) which was expanding away from London. The Great Central's line was engineered to a high standard with a view to it being further extended to link with the proposed Channel Tunnel, in which Watkin also had an interest.

The Manchester to Sheffield line from 1899 thus became host to through express trains to London in competition with the London & North Western and Midland railways.

The original cross–Pennine section and in particular the Worsborough branch were difficult to work with steam traction as freight journeys were slow; the heavier trains required double–heading as well as banking assistance. Much of the central section of the line, between

Hadfield and Penistone, was widened to four tracks, the extensive Up and Down goods lines enabling the slow freights to be overtaken by faster traffic. From early in the 20th century there were thoughts that electric traction, then in its infancy, might be the answer. After the Grouping of the railways in 1922, the new owner, the London & North Eastern Railway, continued to look into this. Electrification was finally authorised in 1936. Progress however was halted by the Second World War, with some electrification infrastructure already in place. Nevertheless during the war the LNER built a locomotive which became No.26000. After the war, this locomotive was given the name TOMMY, and it became the prototype of the Class EM1, later Class 76.

Immediately after Nationalisation, British Railways took on the electrification project, designated Manchester-Sheffield-Wath (MSW) but dropped the pre-war plans to include Manchester (Central) station as one of the extremities. The electrification was to the then national standard of 1500 volts DC. The condition of the Woodhead tunnels was found to be a major problem; after over 100 years of continuous use they were considered to be beyond economic repair. It was therefore decided to build a new by-pass tunnel immediately to the south of the existing bores.

The electrification was implemented in three stages. The first, in 1952, was the Worsborough branch and the main line as far as Dunford Bridge. The eastern limit was the marshalling yard at Wath, about six miles south-east of Barnsley and which had been built by the Great Central in 1907; located virtually in the centre of the South Yorkshire coalfield.

The second stage was from Manchester to Dunford Bridge. In conjunction with this came the opening of the new tunnel at Woodhead. The grand official ceremony was held on 3rd June 1954 and a specially embellished locomotive, No. 26020, which had previously been exhibited at the Festival of Britain in 1951, hauled the official first train on what was proudly heralded as Britain's first electrified main-line.

26020 was one of a class of fifty-seven Bo-Bo locomotives which followed TOMMY and these were designed to haul the majority of the traffic. In addition to conventional vacuum brakes, the locomotives were also fitted with a regenerative braking system for controlling speeds between 16 m.p.h. and 55 m.p.h. This enabled locomotives to feed power back into the electrical system to be used by any ascending trains and was particularly useful for these lines as there were virtually no level stretches. An early modification was to augment these brakes with a rheostat brake for slow speeds, but this was not regenerative.

The MSW line was also provided with seven larger, more powerful Co-Co locomotives (Class EM2) to haul the express passenger trains between the major cities of Manchester and Sheffield, a service which commenced in September 1954. Though these locomotives had superior riding qualities to the EM1s at higher speeds, the overall speed limits imposed due to the curving nature of the route meant their true potential could never be fully exploited.

The route to London, south of Sheffield was downgraded to a secondary line in 1960 when all day-time trains between Manchester and London via Sheffield were discontinued. Stopping passenger trains between Sheffield and Nottingham were withdrawn in 1963. It was finally severed, as a through route, in 1966 but the prospects for the electrified section remained good and it had been recommended for upgrading in the infamous Beeching Report of 1963. The electrification was even extended in the Sheffield area to serve the new marshalling yard at Tinsley, which opened in 1965.

However the recommendations of the Beeching Report were not followed in this instance and the decision was taken to concentrate the Manchester–Sheffield passenger services on the rival former Midland Railway route via the Hope valley and thus Manchester–Sheffield passenger trains, via Woodhead, were withdrawn in January 1970. This left the central section of the line between Hadfield and Penistone without regular passenger trains, though excursions and diverted trains continued to use it. The EM2 locomotives had all been withdrawn shortly prior to this event and they were later sold to the Netherlands State Railway.

During the 1970s the MSW route settled down as nominally 'freight only'. In connection with the new generation of so called 'merry–go–round' (MGR) coal trains which were designed to take coal direct from colliery to power station, thirty of the EM1 locomotives were equipped to work in multiple and were also fitted with train air-braking equipment. A cab-to-cab communication system, using the overhead line, was also installed to assist the operation of banked trains which were still necessary on the Worsborough branch. However, as neither the collieries nor power stations were connected to electric lines, a change of traction from diesel to electric, and then back to diesel, was necessary, thus highlighting a weakness of the system.

We join the story in March 1977 with all but ten of the original fifty-seven production Class 76 locomotives still in service. Due to a general decline in freight traffic, the seemingly unthinkable prospect of closure was being mentioned. The DC electrification was now non-standard, as from

the late 1950s, 25kV AC had been adopted as the overhead electrification standard on Britain's railways. Conversion to AC was estimated to be too costly, and the relatively small – stand-alone – electrification system was now considered to be inefficient due to the need for most of its trains having to be diesel hauled both before and after going under the wires.

Most of the goods loops had been removed by 1977 but the line was still serving as a vital cross-Pennine freight artery and regular passenger diversion route as, ironically, the two lengthy and ageing tunnels on the Hope valley line were by now requiring frequent maintenance. Diesel multiple units were used on the eastern section of the line for local passenger services between Sheffield and Huddersfield and a fleet of eight Class 506, three-car, electric multiple units operated the Manchester to Hadfield and Glossop local services

Woodhead tunnel was still only just over twenty years old and thus presented a modern appearance. However, elsewhere on the system were to be found many signal boxes dating back to the GCR and even the MS&LR, track-side signs of similar vintage and even the occasional GCR signal. The Worsborough branch contained several level crossings and was partly signalled by semaphores. As a system within a system it presented a fascinating study for railway photography.

This is a personal view of the system and does not claim to be comprehensive in its coverage; indeed new angles were still being sought on the last day! Nevertheless, I hope the photographs go some way to providing entertaining glimpses of a unique railway.

(*below*) **Wednesday 8th July 1981, Wortley**: A fine panoramic view of the Yorkshire countryside and the line was available from the A629 road just north of Wortley village. 76011 and 76024 turning to the north-west on the climb approaching Thurgoland tunnel with a loaded train of 21-ton hoppers. The line of trees immediately below the train, hide the meandering River Don which meets the Little Don a short distance away at Deepcar.

1977 - 1979

Monday 7th March 1977, Woodhead: 76053 approached from the west and entered the tunnel with a mixed train including hoppers for alumina silicate and grain. New platforms were erected on the new alignment for the tunnel but the station closed on 27th July 1964, after only ten years service. The old Up and Down line tunnels can be clearly seen to the left of the new tunnel. The modern appearance of the classic tunnel setting is in sharp contrast to much of the remainder of the line.

7th March 1977, Crowden: 76053 returns west with loaded 16-ton mineral wagons, passing the site of Crowden station which closed with effect from 4th February 1957. The mile post indicates the distance from Manchester (Piccadilly) station, formerly London Road, and this sequence continued to Marylebone illustrating that the Great Central Railway went to the south rather than originating from there. (*below*) **7th March 1977, Torside**: 76028 and 76012 head MGR empties over Torside level crossing. The former Great Central signal box awaits its final repaint.

Friday 20ᵗʰ January 1978 Penistone: 76056 passing eastbound, light engine.

(*below*) **Penistone**: It was unusual to see a multiple unit fitted engine working solo but during the final years of the line's operation, anything was possible. MU fitted 76025 passes westbound with a mixed rake.

Penistone: A lone passenger waits on the former Lancashire & Yorkshire Railway Down platform for a train on the branch to Huddersfield. The bleakness of Penistone in winter, located high up in the Pennines, is well illustrated. At least the Up platform has a shelter of sorts.

Penistone: Heading east with another miscellany of wagon types, 76047 approaches the junction with the Huddersfield line. The distinct divisions to this junction station, which once boasted five through platforms, can be seen in this wide-angle view

Friday 17th February 1978, Manchester (Piccadilly): Formerly known as London Road, this station was rebuilt in the early 1960s during which time it was renamed. Immediately prior to Grouping, its joint owners had been the London & North Western Railway and the Great Central Railway - who shared the station but not the platforms. The electrification of the old GC lines to 1500 volt d.c. and the former LNW lines to 25kV a.c. ensured the old boundaries were adhered to! This elevated view shows the four platforms located in the ex GC side.

(*below*) **Manchester (Piccadilly)**: A Class 506 EMU, passing a sister unit, makes a prompt departure with the 1400 to Hadfield.

(*opposite, far left*) **Friday 18th August 1978, Blackmoor Crossing**: This quiet location was on the main line about two miles east of Penistone between Oxspring and Thurgoland. The signal box was of Manchester, Sheffield & Lincolnshire Railway origin and dated from 1878, being a MSL Type 1 design. The original 12-lever frame was replaced by a 20-lever frame in 1956. The box finally closed in May 1983 which coincided with the closure of the line from Deepcar to Penistone.

(*opposite, top right*) **Blackmoor Crossing**: Trackside signs in the name of the Great Central Railway still warned users of the crossing.

(*opposite, bottom*) **Blackmoor Crossing**: A Class 102 diesel multiple unit (DMU) passes the dilapidated signal box with the 1320 service from Sheffield to Huddersfield.

(*above*) **Blackmoor Crossing**: 76003 heads east with a train of 16-ton Merchant Coal Opens (MCOs) otherwise mineral wagons! This visit to the line was rather unwisely timed during the peak holiday season. Therefore, these four illustrations were the only worthwhile photographs taken all day after a totally fruitless venture to the Worsborough branch.

Thursday 8th February 1979, Sheffield: Though Victoria station had closed nine years earlier it was still largely intact. A little animation is added to this panoramic view by a Class 76 passing through the lifeless platforms light engine. The adjoining hotel, which had been nicely spruced-up, dominates the left side of the scene. (*below*) **8th February 1979 Sheffield (Victoria)**: In those less 'Health & Safety' conscious days, access was easily gained and tolerated even though piecemeal demolition was taking place. 76054 once named PLUTO, was one of a batch of twelve of the EM1 class fitted with train heating boilers and which would have regularly hauled passenger trains to this place. Now however, it is reduced to trundling an eastbound rake of empty MCOs through the decaying station remains.

(*right*) **Sheffield (Victoria)**: There were four through platforms and an east facing bay, in addition to two freight avoiding lines. The Down slow platform No.2, which was once subdivided East and West, still displayed memorabilia - the station never had totems.

(*below*) **Sheffield (Victoria)**: Incongruously the Sheffield - Huddersfield trains still passed through. A Class 102 DMU is seen with the 1303 service from Huddersfield to Sheffield. A reversal was necessary at Nunnery Junction before taking the Nunnery chord to reach the former Sheffield (Midland) station.

Sheffield (Victoria): Bay platform No.1 points towards signs of life in the distance. (*below*) Having taken the Down goods line to the north of the platforms, 76040 re-emerges into view with a westbound freight and immediately begins the climb to the Pennines.

(*opposite, top*) **Saturday 21st April 1979, Dinting viaduct:** This was a day when the line saw two railtours. 76046 is seen with the return working from Manchester (Piccadilly) to London (Paddington) with the unusual spectacle of a rake of preserved GWR Didcot-based coaches. The viaduct was strengthened by the Great Central during 1918-19 making it better 'fit for purpose' if rather less aesthetically pleasing. (*opposite*) **Woodhead:** 76030 and 76014 enter the tunnel with the other special which had originated from the North East. This had been worked outbound via the Hope Valley to the Dinting Railway Centre by LNER V2 No.4771 GREEN ARROW. It was taken on from Tinsley by a 'Deltic'. Beat that!

Saturday 27th October 1979: The *TRANS PENNINE FREIGHTER* run by Hertfordshire Railtours originated from London (Euston) and was boarded at Derby with Class 40 No.40067 in charge. EM1s 76027 and 76023 took over at Rotherwood sidings and swiftly accelerated away for the journey to Manchester (Piccadilly). The trip afforded a rare glimpse of the somewhat isolated 79-years old Dunford East signal box (*above*) and a close view (*below*) of Woodhead reservoir as the sun at last came out.

(*right*) **Manchester (Piccadilly)**: The rather cramped scene at the buffer stops as the Class 76s make a rare appearance here. The itinerary handed out on the day caused some consternation as 'diesel haulage' from, and back to Guide Bridge, albeit Class 40, was indicated! So, this opportunity was a bonus.

(*below*) **Manchester (Piccadilly)**: Two different 76s, 76011 and 76025 await departure with the return working. None of the four MSW locomotives used to haul the railtour had been cleaned but then morale amongst the staff on the line was probably not far from rock bottom at this time anyway. Sadly, it was not possible for the tour passengers to get a front view as the turnaround was very brief due to marginal late running. The tour was electrically hauled to Tinsley Yard where 40067 took over to Barnetby. A pair of Class 20s took it on to Cleethorpes before the 40 took the train back south via the East Midlands. This was truly in the spirit of the Manchester Sheffield & Lincolnshire Railway.

(above & below) **Penistone:** A photo stop was made here. By now the Down platform buildings had been demolished creating a rather barren appearance compared to a few months earlier. The signalman in Huddersfield Junction signal box is well placed to keep a watchful gaze on the travellers safely occupying the running lines, but would it be allowed these days?

1980 - The Last Full Year Of Operation

Thursday 13th March 1980, Darnall: The ambitions for this trip are long forgotten but the return of just two 'electric' photographs was very poor though perhaps partly explained by the strike in the steel industry at that time. (*above*) With the entrance to the former engine shed on the left, and the Cravens factory on the right, a reasonably clean 76051 heads for Rotherwood with empty hoppers. (*below*) With the train approaching the small island platform station on a quadrupled line, we get a tantalising glimpse of what might have been had the Great Central's London Extension been electrified rather than closed.

Friday 6th June 1980, Worsborough Bridge Crossing: A view looking east beyond the Great Central Type 5b box. The track here was in a pronounced dip due to mining subsidence. It would be interesting to know if the catenary cross members had ever been altered and adjusted to allow for the vertical ground movements which may have taken place during the near thirty years operation of the electrified railway in this area. (*below*) **6th June 1980, Lewden Crossing**: A general view showing the low crossing box and also Great Central signs still warning would be trespassers. The signal box was even older being a MS&L Type 2 design. These were two of five level crossings located within a space of a few miles on the branch.

(*above & below*) **6th June 1980, Glasshouse Crossing**: Small box, large letters! This was another crossing on the Worsborough branch. Note the precautions in place to warn drivers of high vehicles of the hazard ahead. A rail-served steel works once occupied the vacant site to the south-west of the crossing.

6th June 1980, Thurlstone: A panoramic view looking west with a pair of Class 76s taking a mixed freight of 16-ton MCOs, 21-ton hoppers, covered hoppers and steel carriers over the crossing at Shore Hall having rounded the curve at Bullhouse. (*below*) A little while later, just to the east, another pairing consisting 76016 and 76025 roll past the Great Central signal box with a train of empty 21-ton hoppers.

6th June 1980, Woodhead: 76053 passes the signal box and the erstwhile station platform with a cosmopolitan variety of opens, hoppers and steel carriers. (*below*) 76038 and 76035 emerge into the sunlight with yet another MGR for Fiddler's Ferry.

6th June 1980, Bullhouse: A few hours later, 76035 and 76038 return to Wath from Godley Junction with an empty MGR. The arch for the long defunct Down goods is clearly seen. (*below*) MU fitted 76025, 76016, 76024 and 76015 make an unusual spectacle working 'light' to the west. Note that each locomotive has at least one pantograph raised.

(*left*) **6th June 1980, Thurgoland Tunnel**: A Class 110 DMU with the 1538 service from Sheffield to Leeds is seen emerging from the new tunnel constructed for the electrification. The original two-track tunnel had insufficient clearance for the overhead catenary but, unlike its longer counterparts at Woodhead, it was still in good condition and was thus retained for the Up line.

(*below*) **Tuesday 2nd October 1980, Valehouse**: Heading east with a train of empty 21-ton hoppers, a pair of Class 76s blend in well with the wonderful scenery of Longdendale.

2nd October 1980, Wadsley Bridge: This delightful station was three miles north-west of Sheffield (Victoria). It had closed to regular traffic on 15th June 1959 but was used for general excursions until 1965 and, being convenient for Sheffield Wednesday's Hillsborough stadium, continued to be retained for football specials into the 1990s. In 1980 it was still complete with its Eastern Region running in boards and had modern lighting. At the south end was a Great Central Type 4 signal box which added to the station's very traditional appearance. A rare Class 40 visitor, vacuum braked 40009, 'whistles' down the grade in a south-easterly direction with empty 16-ton mineral wagons (MCOs).

Wadsley Bridge: 76016, an air-braked example of Class 76, thus more normally seen in multiple, climbs past the signal box with a rake of 16-ton MCOs.

Wadsley Bridge: (*above*) There were two of these signs, at either end of the station. The totems had long since been removed but at least one (*below*) survives in preservation.

Wadsley Bridge: The small yard located on the Down side still had a Great Central signal and this was pulled off for photographic purposes during a lull in activity on the main line. (*below*) The friendly signalman enjoys a few brief moments of sunshine as a Class 110 DMU rushes through with the 1538 from Sheffield to Leeds. Besides the yard facilities at the west end of the station, Wadsley Bridge had a goods shed at its eastern end too.

Wadsley Bridge: 76016 makes a quick return, light engine to the east.

Wadsley Bridge: 76029 and 76011 are about to cross the A61 road bridge as they approach up the gradient with the British Oxygen Company train of 100-ton tanks conveying compressed oxygen from Broughton Lane to Ditton.

Wadsley Bridge: 76038 and 76033 bring 16-ton mineral empties east.

Wadsley Bridge: 76054, with a mixed freight which includes a road vehicle, ascends the 1 in 132 gradient to the west, concluding this photographic session.

Wednesday 29ᵗʰ October 1980, Thurlstone Crossing: 27 miles east of Manchester, according to the milepost. 76054 is seen again, this time travelling east 'light engine' and allowing a view of the attractive setting for the line and Shore Hall crossing in the distance. 'Light engine' movements, reflecting un-balanced workings due to the decline in traffic, were a common occurrence by this time.(*below*) The 81 years old Great Central Type 5a signal box, by now with a pronounced backwards lean! It would require more than lick of paint to bring the appearance of this box up to a reasonable standard but that was never going to happen.

29th October 1980, Dunford Bridge: This was the much less photogenic and therefore less photographed eastern end of Woodhead tunnel. 76010 and 76016 head a loaded MGR (*above*) through the long closed station and into the tunnel (*below*). It fell to this pair of Bo-Bos to take the very last train of all, a Speedlink service from Harwich to Trafford Park, through the tunnel during the early hours on Saturday 18th July 1981.

Sunday 30th November 1980: (*above & below*) On winter Sundays the line took on a different character as it resumed its role as a passenger line even hosting London and Manchester expresses: one in either direction. Type 4 Class 47 47543 is in charge of the 0746 from London (St Pancras) to Manchester (Piccadilly) and is passing through the abandoned Sheffield (Victoria), allowing good views of the freight avoiding lines on the north side of the station. The Great Central signal box - Sheffield No.4 - dated from 1902 and by this time had the added responsibility of signalling trains using the link, created in 1965, from Sheffield (Midland).

(*above*) **Dunford Bridge**: Low sun, a smattering of snow on the ground. Winter has arrived at Dunford Bridge.

(*right*) **Guide Bridge:** The Great Central Railway was often at the forefront of implementing schemes to achieve efficiencies in signalling. When the widening of the section of line between Ardwick and Hyde Junction in the Manchester area was carried out in the very early 1900s, power signalling, based on the principle of a low pressure pneumatic system, was introduced. This resulted in a reduction of both the number of signal boxes and levers required to control a given location. That system had originated in the United States and had been adopted in Britain by the London & South Western Railway whose signal design was closely followed by the GCR. The system was later converted to electro-pneumatic. An operating cylinder for the home signal can just be seen on this lattice post - between the two arms - which was worked by Guide Bridge East box and controlled the movements on the Down Goods whereas the distant belonged to Ashton Junction. That route indicator was a later addition. Guide Bride East was abolished in November 1984.

Manchester (Piccadilly): (*above*) 47543 on arrival. The silver roof was a Stratford depot trademark and evokes memories of the long standing daily boat train from Harwich via Woodhead which once terminated here. (below) Appropriately a Class 124 Trans-Pennine DMU with a service to Hull awaits the 1500 departure time at platform 3.

(*opposite, top*) **Tuesday 30th December 1980, Deepcar**: This station was eight miles from Sheffield (Victoria) and, like Wadsley Bridge, closed on Monday 15th June 1959. The line from Sheffield is still retained for trip workings serving the steel works at Stocksbridge which is situated at the end of a two-mile long branch off the former main line. However sights such as 76014 and 76007 attacking the 1 in 130 gradient with a westbound unfitted loaded coal train are long gone. (*opposite, bottom*) The signal box diagram showing the branch and sidings. Courtesy of another friendly signalman, who also provided a very welcome hot drink.

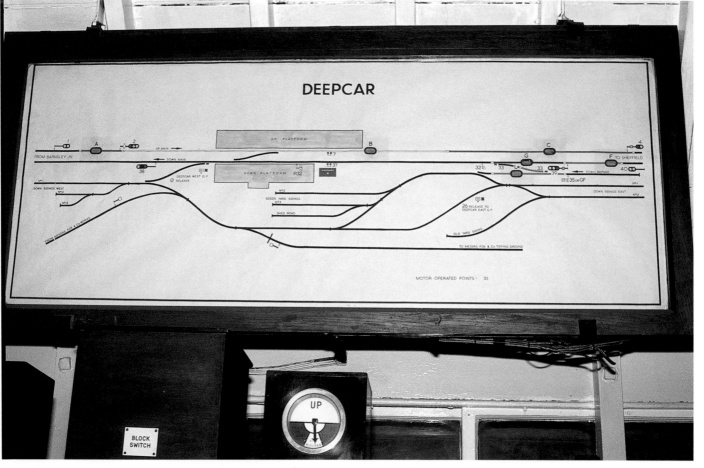

(*opposite, top and bottom*) **Deepcar**: 76011 and 76029 with another westbound unfitted coal train going slow enough to allow a change of position to capture the brake van passing the signal box. This was a MS&L Type 3 design, moved here from another location in 1906. The substantial station buildings add a Gothic touch to the scene.

Deepcar: The prime reason of this visit is revealed as 76006 passes with the *XMAS TOMMY RAILTOUR*. This was run by the LCGB and originated from Liverpool being electrically hauled from Manchester (Piccadilly) as far as Rotherwood sidings. Note the 16-ton mineral wagons (MCOs) still serving the local coal merchants. The catenary equipped sidings enabled 76s to shunt. This location lives on in its full electrification glory in 4mm scale model form thanks to the Nottingham Model Railway Society, and often appears at exhibitions.

West Silkstone Junction: While the rail tour was being diesel hauled away from the wires directly to Wath, 76006 retraced its route to Penistone and then reversed to proceed down the Worsborough branch to take it over again. The signal box was a MS&L Type 1 design, opened in 1880 and subsequently extended at the west end. Though passenger trains between Barnsley and Penistone now pass here, with the closure of the branch there was no need for a signal box and this closed in August 1981. Note that the base is of brick rather than timber construction, unusual on this side of Woodhead.

Worsborough Bank: (*below*) In the gathering gloom of the December afternoon, 76054 provides assistance to 76006 on the steepest section of the incline approaching Silkstone No.2 tunnel. In 1981, the final tour, the *EASTER TOMMY* was advertised and then shown as cancelled causing it to be missed as the subsequent news that it was 'on again' eluded me. For the record 76025 hauled this train over the full length of the main line but the Worsborough branch was not included in the itinerary.

Winter and Spring 1981

Tuesday 10th February 1981, Penistone: On hearing of snowfall, a day's leave was hastily obtained to capture some wintry scenes. Due to unfounded fears about the state of the roads the trip was undertaken from the East Midlands by train. An early success at Penistone was the capture of 76023 and 76022 which had followed the DMU from Sheffield with a loaded coal train comprising 16-ton MCOs.

Oughty Bridge signal box had been photographed from the train.

Penistone Gᴅs: 76007 and 76026 approaching with an eastbound mixed freight of mainly empties.

Penistone Gds: A Christmas card scene? 76009 and 76014 pass the box heading east with covered hoppers.

Penistone Gds: 76024 and 76006 have rather more work to do, albeit quietly, lifting a loaded MGR up the 1 in 130 gradient.

Bullhouse: 76031 and 76033 sweep beneath the overbridge with more MGR empties. This is the train also illustrated on the front cover.

Shore Hall Crossing: In fading light and facing a two mile walk back to Penistone station, Bullhouse was reluctantly left without seeing a west bound freight. However, very shortly afterwards whilst en route, 76008 and 76021 were photographed with a loaded MGR.

Tuesday 7ᵗʰ April 1981, Broadbottom: By this date closure in the summer had been confirmed and there were even rumours that diesels would take over for the last few months. It was therefore with some relief that 76015 and 76014 were seen heading west 'light engine'. Four original Great Central platform seats are visible. (*below*) The newly cleaned station buildings and bridge provide an attractive backdrop for a Class 506 EMU arriving with the 1200 from Manchester (Piccadilly) to Hadfield.

(*left*) **7ᵗʰ April 1981, Godley Junction**: Close up of 76033's cab; with 76031, the Bo-Bo was waiting in the Liverpool line platform to take over a train.

(*below*) **Godley Junction**: A comparison in styles as a Class 506 EMU arrives with the 1530 from Manchester (Piccadilly). Brookfold signal box, just down the branch line, had been switched-out four months previously when the branch was taken out of use pending formal closure, hence the apparently rather alarming conflicting signal to the rear of the light engines.

(*opposite*) **Godley Junction**: With closure looming, small clusters of enthusiasts were to be found at most major locations. (*top*) There are no prizes for guessing the topic of conversation as the driver waiting in the cab of 76031 forcibly makes a point to the small audience. (*bottom*) Later, 76033 and 76031 had backed onto an empty freight which had been brought in by 40196 and are awaiting departure for the east as 76006 and 76024 bring a westbound freight in the opposite direction. This was also the locomotive changeover point for eastbound MGR empties. The Great Central signal box remained in use until 1984, several years after the demise of the junction. The inconveniently sited station closed in 1995, having been replaced by a new station better located for the local community.

7th April 1981, Guide Bridge: 76006 and 76024 attract some interest as they pass through westbound and 'light'. The building on the left in the lower illustration contained the MSW crew manning offices from where the Woodhead route was basically 'organised'.

Guide Bridge: Still a significant junction, Guide Bridge had been a stabling point for Class 76s for many years, but the demise of steam saw a specific yard created (in the distance between the '40' and the box) for the electric locomotives and other motive power. 40022 once named LACONIA drags a westbound freight past Ashton Junction signal box. (*below*) 40096 passes through in the opposite direction with a rake of stone hoppers bound for one of the Buxton quarries.

(*above*) **Guide Bridge**: The 1715 six-car service from Manchester (Piccadilly) arrives.

(*left*) **Wednesday 27th May 1981, Rotherwood Exchange Sidings**: This was the eastern limit of the MSW electrification. Nearest the camera are 76051 and 76008, with coupled pairs 76026 and 76013, 76023 and 76022, in the distance awaiting their next turn of duty.

(*opposite, top*) **Thursday 28th May 1981, Manchester (Piccadilly)**: A Class 506 EMU awaits the 1200 departure time.

(*opposite*) **28th May 1981, Hadfield**: In the distance a westbound working with 76011 and 76009 is held until the Class 506 EMU has departed with the 1413 service to Manchester (Piccadilly). The single platform at Hadfield served both arrivals and departures, and was the eastern boundary of the suburban passenger services from Manchester. The cessation of the through passenger services between Sheffield (Victoria) and Manchester in 1970 removed the requirement for Up and Down platforms here, hence the simplified layout.

Hadfield: In showery conditions 76011 and 76009 resume their journey with a loaded coal train comprising 16-ton mineral wagons and 24-ton hoppers. (*below*) The following service from Manchester (Piccadilly) arrives. New signalling for permanent single line working, which would have been introduced anyway once this had become the end of the line, awaits commissioning.

Hadfield to Dinting: This location had been the scene of a serious derailment of an Up freight train on 10th March 1981 as a result of which the Up main and Up goods loop were severely damaged, never to be repaired! Single line working over the Down main was therefore implemented. A further less damaging derailment occurred on 8th April when a tanker train became partially derailed while regaining the Up line at Hadfield.

Dinting: A Class 506 EMU with the 1430 from Manchester (Piccadilly) to Hadfield nevertheless takes the branch platform, for a prior visit trip to Glossop. (*below*) 76022 and 76023 gingerly bring a long, unfitted freight over the, conveniently situated, facing cross-over and on to the Down line, to work wrong-line as far as Hadfield. The damage to track and the Down platform is clearly visible.

Summer 1981 - The Final Workings

Wednesday 10th June 1981, Elsecar Junction, Wath: In order to avoid potentially wasting time on the Worsborough branch, a strategy was adopted to visit Wath first to see if there were likely to be any trains up the branch. This location was found to be very rewarding in its own right. 76038 and 76039 enter the yard in preparation for a trip up the incline. The line off to the left served Elsecar Main and Corton Wood collieries. (*below*) The pair look on as Type 5 diesel 56004 powers through on the Down goods with a northbound MGR for the Aire valley. This train will no doubt be worked by the same locomotive throughout and thus has no need to visit the yard. This illustrates the perceived inefficiency of the electrified system in the diesel era.

(*above*) **Elsecar Junction, Wath**: 76039 and 76038 leave in the late morning with an MGR for Fiddlers Ferry.

(*left*) **Oxspring Tunnel**: The sun disappeared before 76039 and 76038 came past but was fortunately still out when 76013 and 76026 travelled east slightly earlier with an empty MGR.

(*opposite, top*) **10th June 1981, Oughty Bridge**: A small yard remained here although the station had closed to passengers, as with the others between Sheffield and Penistone, on 15th June 1959. After the closure of the Woodhead route above Penistone, the Great Central Type 4 signal box located at this place lingered on for a little while longer as this section of line remained open until the diversion of the passenger service via Barnsley in 1983. With Wharncliffe wood dominating the background, two of Tinsley's English Electric Type 1s, 20128 and 20060, proceed east down the gradient from Stocksbridge with an unfitted freight consisting loaded 21-ton plate wagons and empty 16-ton mineral opens. (*centre*) 76051 climbs past the goods yard with a train of 16-ton mineral wagons and 21-ton hoppers for Stocksbridge. (*bottom*) A Class 101 DMU with the 1718 from Huddersfield to Sheffield passes the signal box. Note the well used and still electrified sidings.

10th June 1981, Dunford Bridge: A panoramic view showing the general scene at the eastern end of the Woodhead tunnel. A temporary village for the personnel involved in driving the new tunnel was established on the moors above.

Dunford Bridge: (*above*) 76039 and 76038 westbound with the same MGR seen leaving the yard at Wath earlier in the day. (*below*) The Dunford West signal box diagram. A gradient profile on the top right revealed the ascent from the east portal to a point just over a mile inside was 1 in 1186 rising. The gradient from the western portal was 1 in 130 for two miles inside! The Up and Down loops survived to the end.

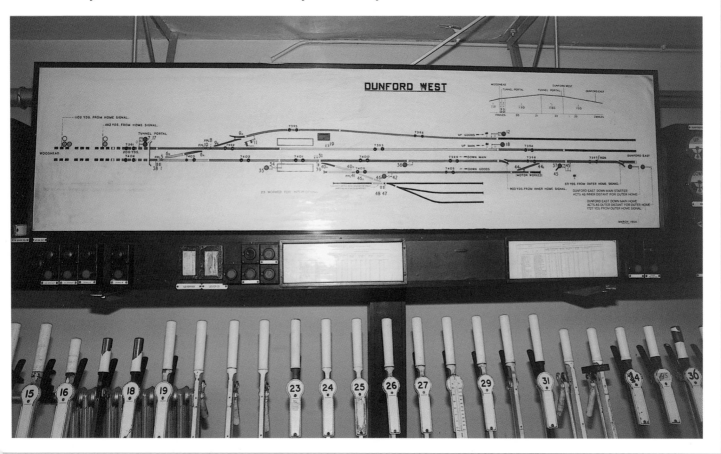

Dunford Bridge: 76023 and 76022 bring another loaded MGR westwards through the station. (*below*) A telephoto view into the tunnel. The old single bore tunnels each rose on a gradient of 1 in 201 to a summit at the eastern portal, whereas in the new tunnel the steeper climb from Woodhead achieved a summit roughly two-thirds of the way into the tunnel, clearly seen from the lights. This would have safely allowed two trains on each line, with suitable adjustment to the signalling, if it was ever felt necessary to increase line capacity. In the event this was never achieved and the tunnel remained as a single block section.

Thursday 2nd July 1981, Dunford Bridge: During the summer the number of enthusiasts visiting the line increased and a signalman at Dunford Bridge was particularly welcoming. During a not uncommon lull in traffic, permission was given for the tunnel portal to be explored. The twin signals are for the Up goods loop and Up main.

Dunford Bridge: Meanwhile, at other times, it was business as usual as 76010 and 76016 bring another loaded MGR towards the station. (*below*) No doubt the driver of 76031 and 76037, with yet another westbound MGR, was bemused to find his train routed through the Down goods loop. This move was set up by the signalman to provide something different for the assembled photographers.

2nd July 1981, Glasshouse Crossing.

Three chronological views of the train engines and the banking pair as they approach, and pass the signal box and level crossing: 76034 and 76032, assisted in the rear by 76031 and 76037, lift another Fiddlers Ferry MGR up the Worsborough branch which was rising at 1 in 103 at this point. All too soon this everyday scene would become pure history.

Wednesday 8ᵗʰ July 1981, Wombwell Main: (*this page, above*) A chance meeting with an enthusiast who was having a ride in the cab of one of the banking engines seen at Glasshouse crossing, alerted me to the fact that such unofficial rides seemed to be available 'on application'. On a bright morning 76038 and 76039 await the train from Wath. (*below*) This duly arrives hauled by 76012 and 76007. (*opposite, top*) 76038 and 76039 have moved onto the rear of the train. (*opposite bottom*) **West Silkstone Junction**: Job done!

West Silkstone Junction – Wombwell Main: All clear from West Silkstone Junction's starter at the mouth of the 289 yards long Silkstone No.1 tunnel as viewed from the cab of 76038. (*below*) Passing Worsboro Bridge Crossing, Glasshouse Crossing's tall home signal is clearly visible just round the distant curve. The locomotives were in regenerative mode at this point but as there were no ascending trains nearby the current generated would be wasted.

Wombwell Main: 76033 was also on banking duty that day.

Wombwell Main: 76016 and 76010, heading east 'light engines', pass 76038 and 76039 which await their next turn.

8th July 1981, Woodhead: The signal box was by now switched out, which allowed the opportunity of some different angles for the small group of enthusiasts. Taken from the signal box steps, 76010 and 76016, seen earlier in the day, leave the tunnel with another loaded MGR from Wath. (*below*) At this late stage it was a case of savouring moments like this: 76027 and 76025 leave the tunnel with another freight.

Woodhead: 76016 and 76010 are observed yet again, with eastbound MGR empties passing the deserted signal box.

Woodhead: Framed by the tunnel mouth, 76011 is seen emerging. For the record, 76024 was the coupled locomotive and the pair were heading a freight.

Friday, 17th July 1981: The Final Day of Full Operation.

Friday 17th July 1981, Elsecar Junction: And so to the last full day. On a bright morning, weather-wise at least, 76010 and 76016 arrive light from Wath depot. (*below*) They come back over the level crossing. The line here remained open and the signal box survived until November 1985. But this was the beginning of the end.

Wath Yard: For this last day there seemed to be no restrictions on entering the yard. And so, with a few others, advantage was taken to obtain photographs of what was to be the penultimate electrically hauled train waiting to depart. The stock for the last MGR over the MSW route is stabled alongside 76010 and 76016.

Wath Yard: Another view just prior to departure.

Elsecar Junction: 76010 and 76016 which, less than 24-hours later, would go down in history as the last locomotives to work a freight through Woodhead tunnel (76016 was also one of the first pair back in 1954) make their departure from Wath.

Elsecar Junction: The pair head north towards Adlam Junction where they will veer to the west to commence their last ever ascent of the Worsborough branch. If only locomotives could talk! (*below*) **Gilroyd**: 76010 and 76016 are seen crossing the M1 motorway, climbing the 1 in 105, about a mile away from the start of the 1 in 40 section. This hastily chosen location was visited in the hope of getting a clear view of the whole train. It would have been nice to have been able to try it again in winter. Nevertheless, the sharp-eyed might spot 76007 (just to the right of the colliery headgear) bringing up the rear, with the hidden 76012; Kendall Green's Up distant too. The remaining working life of this section of line could be best measured in minutes, rather than hours, at this time and this would be a disused railway by the afternoon. The bridge remains as a prominent landmark on the M1, forming the link over the motorway for the Dove Valley Trail between Silkstone Common and Wombwell - it is well worth a visit to walk the track bed of one of the steeper sections of the MSW system. The glimpse of the headstocks of the long closed mine is a poignant reminder that coal mining and the Woodhead route, and in particular the Worsborough branch, were intrinsically linked; their mutual decline being no co-incidence.

Oxspring Viaduct: No luck with the sun here as 76010 and 76016 continue their journey, the unrelenting climb having eased to 1 in 100 at this point. (*below*) **Bullhouse**: A final visit to this favourite location. 76032 and 76034 sweep past with what was the last electrically hauled MGR of all from Wath yard. Note that the track bed is in immaculate condition. The Worsborough branch having closed at lunchtime, after one further light engine working following this train, had its signal boxes stripped of their highly collectable equipment before nightfall!

Mottram: An attempt was made to get here before the 76s had come off their train but they had already gone when this photograph was taken. The MGR awaits a diesel locomotive to take it to its destination. The following week these wagons would be diesel hauled throughout, via a different route. The reception sidings for this yard, built by the LNER in the 1930s, still served as the locomotive change point for these trains. Meanwhile it is just another day for the Class 506 EMU passing with the 1243 service from Hadfield. The rain clouds perhaps sum up the mood rather better than the sunny morning.

Torside: Unfortunately, and somewhat inevitably, heavy rain set in around lunchtime and Torside was felt to be the best place to be as the car could provide shelter between trains. 76016 and 76010, on what was a busy day for them; work an empty MGR towards Woodhead in the pouring rain.

Torside: (*opposite, top*) 76022, which was now separated from its long-term partner 76023, takes a scrap metal train east past the box. The 76 managed to keep its BR crest to the end.

(*opposite, bottom*) In much improved conditions, 76051 takes an empty train of 24-ton hoppers off to Yorkshire.

(*above*) Another view of 76051 as it heads east, ascending the 1 in 117 gradient.

(*below*) Some weak sunshine illuminates 76006 and 76014 working west with HEA coal hoppers. Later in the evening these locomotives worked the very last loaded MGR, taking a train west from Barnsley Junction, Penistone.

Torside: 76010 and 76016 work another loaded MGR westwards. The signal box here, the third such box to stand on the site, was a Great Central Type 5a, dating from 1909, but this was now the penultimate shift. (*below*) The inevitable light engine movements were poignant as some were almost certainly their last workings, back to Reddish depot for storage. A lonely 76022 provides my last image of an EM1 on the move in the early evening of that fateful Friday, 17th July 1981!

Postscript

It was agreed, with the unions, that the main line would be left in situ but dismantling of the Worsborough branch commenced with immediate effect of closure.

The Sheffield to Huddersfield DMU service continued to use the route as far as Penistone until May 1983 when the service was diverted via Barnsley. In reality this only involved, the closure of just over a further four miles of the route as the line remains open as far as Deepcar for Stocksbridge steel traffic. Wadsley Bridge continued to see the occasional football special but these withered away in the 1990s.

On a more positive note, passenger services therefore resumed on the former electrified section between Barnsley Junction and the site of West Silkstone Junction.

The Class 506 EMUs continued plying their trade between Manchester and Hadfield until withdrawal in December 1984 when the route was converted to 25kV AC. The pro rata cost of this was significantly less than the estimate produced in 1981 for the whole route! Meanwhile, by this time, track lifting on the main line had commenced.

76020 restored as 26020 and is now part of the National Collection. Six of the seven EM2s continued to provide good service in the Netherlands until 1986. 27000 ELECTRA is preserved at the Midland Railway Centre, Butterley. 27001 ARIADNE is in the Manchester Museum of Science & Industry, in its Dutch livery, and 27003 DIANA is similarly preserved in the Netherlands.

Plans have recently been announced for the electrification of the cross-Pennine route between Leeds and Manchester. Another, the Hope valley line, is to receive significant investment. Later this decade overhead wires should once again reach Sheffield when the Midland Main Line, too, is electrified.

Sunday 23rd July 1995, Midland Railway Centre, Butterley: EM2 E27000 ELECTRA one of the MSW's seven Co-Co passenger locomotives has been beautifully restored, complete with added embellishments and one or two changes from its days working on the railways of the Netherlands.

(*left*) **Thursday 11ᵗʰ August 1983, Oxspring**: A Class 110 DMU with 1035 Sheffield to Huddersfield service, now via Barnsley, leaves the tunnel. Two years on from the end of electric workings, the line has reverted to single track, as built.

(*below*) **Oxspring**: No problem with the sun on this occasion as the 1110 Huddersfield to Sheffield DMU crosses the impressive viaduct.

(*opposite, top*) **Monday 18ᵗʰ October 1993, Hadfield**: Now the end of the line. The conversion from DC to AC is not visibly apparent.

(*opposite, bottom*) **18ᵗʰ October 1993, Glossop**: Commercial development has taken some of the station. A Class 305 25kV EMU waits with the 1108 service from Hadfield to Manchester (Piccadilly).

Wednesday 29ᵗʰ October 1980, Dinting viaduct: The sun sets, as a pair of Class 76s head east.

(*Rear cover*) On Thursday 3ʳᵈ June 1954, EM1 26020 was used to officially open the new Woodhead tunnel. A much published contemporary photograph taken from inside the tunnel mouth revealed the locomotive just about to embark on the historic journey. In 1987 the view from the tunnel was much changed, with track and all overhead catenary removed. Fortunately, 26020 is now preserved in the National Railway Museum's collection and is seen here in the main hall at York.

Acknowledgements

David Christie and Simon Jones – both established photographers when I was starting out. Their slide evenings were a great inspiration.
Hayden Reed – without his invaluable help and encouragement this book would not have come about.
Nick Quinn – for providing information for some of the captions.
David Birch – for technical assistance.
David Allen – for taking this project on.
John Hooper – for supplementing some captions and creating a book.
Finally – To all the railway workers who provided facilities for enjoyment of the railway or simply turned a blind eye at the appropriate time.

Bibliography

An Illustrated Historical Survey of a Great Provincial Station Manchester London Road – compiled by John Hooper – Challenger Publications.
An Illustrated History of the Woodhead Route – Alan Whitehouse – OPC.
A Pictorial Record of LNER Constituent Signalling – A.A.Maclean – OPC.
Great Central: (vols. 1-3) – George Dow – Ian Allan.
Main Line Across the Pennines – C.M.Corroy and A.R.Kaye – Lowlander Publications.
Passengers No More – G.Daniels and L.Dench – Ian Allan.
Profile of the 76s and 77s – David Maxey – OPC.
Rail Centres: Sheffield – Stephen Batty – Ian Allan.
Scenes from the Past 29:Woodhead (vols. 1-3) – E.M.Johnson – Foxline.
Signal Box Register Vol.3 LNER (Southern Area) – Signalling Record Society.